A. NONSO DIKE

Futsal Fun

10 Ways to Empower Working-Class Parents and Student-Athletes, Revolutionizing After-School Routines

This book was professionally typeset on Reedsy.
Find out more at reedsy.com

"To the dedicated Futsal Hearts (fans), working-class parents, student-athletes, families, and communities—this book is a heartfelt tribute to your unwavering spirit, resilience, hope, and love. Gratitude to God's guiding grace. Join us on this empowering journey where families thrive and futsal sparks inspiration. Thank you for being part of this vibrant community.
Keep walking...
only blessings ahead..."

Contents

1

Introduction:

Welcome to "Futsal Fun: Bridging the Gap in Afterschool Sports Programs," an immersive guide shaped by my experiences in early childhood and after-school sports. I'm Anistetus Nonso Dike, thrilled to walk you through the journey that birthed this groundbreaking book.

Embark on a global odyssey, exploring after-school sports programs in Nigeria, South Africa, the Cayman Islands, and Canada. I'll reveal the challenges faced by working-class parents, particularly those tethered to the 9 am to 5 pm grind, and the consequential impact on their student-athlete children. This exploration unravels the profound influence of after-school sports on my formative years, molding not just my character but also sparking a fervor for the dynamic game of futsal.

We'll delve into the heart of my passion for futsal, a sport transcending all traditional boundaries. Uncover the unique technical skills and unbridled joy it bestows upon players. I'll share my connection with the game, narrating how its fast-paced, skill-oriented nature enraptured me early on and transformed futsal from a mere sport into a way of life.

In the core of "Futsal Fun," we'll unveil how this guide acts as a beacon for working-class parents navigating challenges in after-school and school-age sports programs. Tailored for those adhering to the typical 9 am to 5 pm schedule, we'll explore their struggles and present practical solutions to bridge the gap. This chapter serves as your guide to unlocking a new era of after-school empowerment for both parents and their student-athlete children.

As we navigate "Futsal Fun," anticipate a seamless blend of personal narratives, expert insights, and practical solutions. This book goes beyond futsal; it's a comprehensive guide addressing the needs of working-class parents. Expect to discover the keys to enhancing the after-school experience for student-athlete children.

2

Kicking Off a Healthier Lifestyle:

Futsal isn't just a game; it's a trans-formative force that catalyzes a healthier lifestyle, instilling positive habits and promoting overall well-being. In this chapter, we delve into the profound impact of futsal on shaping healthy choices, drawing inspiration from personal experiences that illuminate the connection between dynamic sports and a balanced life.

Growing up as a student-athlete in the after-school arena, I quickly learned that engaging in futsal wasn't merely about scoring goals on the court; it was a holistic journey that extended into my daily life. One crucial aspect that became evident was the integration of healthy nutrition into my routine. Futsal, with its demanding nature, requires sustained energy and endurance. This realization prompted me to explore the world of nutritious foods, discovering the vital role they played in enhancing my performance on the futsal court.

As a student-athlete, the after-school period became a well-structured routine. First and foremost, completing homework before hitting the futsal court was a non-negotiable priority. This disciplined approach

3

not only ensured academic responsibilities were met but also set the stage for a focused and stress-free futsal experience. The after-school center, equipped with tutors and mentors, played a pivotal role in facilitating this balanced routine. Their guidance not only helped me manage time efficiently but also reinforced the importance of academic diligence alongside sporting pursuits.

Futsal, in this context, was akin to a dessert – a reward for completing my homework chores. The joy of engaging in physical sports became a sweet reward, much like relishing a scoop of ice cream after a wholesome meal. This perspective not only transformed the way I approached homework but also nurtured a positive attitude toward combining mental and physical activities seamlessly.

Moreover, the disciplined approach cultivated through after-school routines extended beyond the court. Heading back home with my parents after an invigorating futsal session, the positive effects rippled through family dynamics. The energy and enthusiasm carried from the sports arena infused a lively spirit into our evenings. The bond forged during futsal sessions spilled over into quality family time, fostering communication, and strengthening familial connections.

As a catalyst for a healthier lifestyle, Futsal went beyond the physical aspect. It became a conduit for learning valuable life skills such as time management, discipline, and the significance of a balanced routine. The after-school experience, centered around futsal, became a holistic educational journey that shaped not just my athletic abilities but also my character and approach to life.

In summary, this first point explores the multifaceted impact of futsal on promoting a healthier lifestyle. From the integration of nutritious choices to the disciplined approach of completing homework before play, futsal became a cornerstone in shaping positive habits. The after-school environment, with its supportive tutors and mentors, played a crucial role in fostering this holistic approach. Ultimately, futsal was not just a physical activity but a lifestyle that influenced choices, habits, and family dynamics, making it a powerful catalyst for a balanced and healthier way of life.

3

The ABCs of Skill Development:

A Holistic Approach Through Futsal.

In the dynamic realm of futsal, skill development takes center stage, sculpting young athletes into agile and proficient players. This chapter delves into the fundamental aspects of skill development within the futsal environment, illuminating the trans-formative journey from my childhood playing days in Nigeria to coaching experiences in Canada, Cayman, and South Africa.

During my formative years in Nigeria, futsal became the canvas on which my fundamental skills were intricately painted. The after-school coach, cognizant of the critical role of skill acquisition, cultivated an environment that nurtured not just athletic prowess but also holistic development. In the confined spaces of the futsal court, I not only honed agility and ball control but also grasped the intricacies of the game, laying the foundation for a lifelong passion for the sport.

Fast forward to my coaching days in Canada, Cayman, and South Africa, where the privilege of guiding the next generation of student-athletes allowed me to integrate my coaching philosophy deeply rooted in Early Childhood Education (ECE) principles. Embracing the philosophy of P.I.L.E.S - Physical, Intellectual, Language, Emotional, and Social Development, I witnessed the accelerated growth of fundamental and technical skills in the youth under my guidance.

The futsal after-school environment emerged as a natural incubator for learning, aligning seamlessly with my belief in the holistic development of individuals. The small spaces and specialized court surfaces of futsal not only facilitated constant ball touches but also played a pivotal role in the unconscious and subliminal development of skills. Body mechanics adjusted instinctively, movements ingrained into muscle memory, and quick thinking became second nature as players navigated the swift-paced dynamics of the futsal court. This dynamic setting proved invaluable, laying the groundwork for players to seamlessly transition into becoming technically adept soccer players on the larger field.

Beyond the immediate benefits on the court, the skills acquired in the futsal and after-school environment transcended into daily life. The cognitive and mental skills honed through quick decision-making on the futsal court translated into enhanced problem-solving abilities off the field. Teamwork, a cornerstone of futsal, extended beyond the court into after-school friendships, fostering a sense of community and support that echoes the collaborative spirit of the game.

The profound impact of the futsal and after-school environment extends beyond the realm of sports—it becomes interwoven with the fabric of a young athlete's character. The platform serves as a holistic learning ground where individuals unconsciously carry the acquired skills into various facets of their lives. The benefits manifest not only in the proficiency of well-executed futsal moves but also in the resilience, teamwork, and adaptability displayed in everyday situations.

In a nutshell, this second point reflects on experiences across diverse countries and cultures, the significant benefits and fundamental development skills offered by the futsal and after-school platforms are unmistakable. The synergy between skill development, cognitive growth, and character building creates a comprehensive educational journey. My exploration and observations through early childhood after-school playing days and coaching experiences underscore the trans-formative power of futsal in shaping youth into skilled, resilient, and well-rounded individuals.

4

Teamwork Makes the Dream Work:

In the vibrant world of futsal, the spotlight shifts to the significance of teamwork—a facet that not only shapes game-play but also instills crucial values that reverberate far beyond the court. This chapter delves into the essence of teamwork in futsal, unveiling how it becomes a catalyst for fostering family dynamics, refining social skills, and creating a collaborative environment in the after-school setting.

The courts of futsal are arenas where teamwork transforms into an art form. As players synchronize their movements, anticipate each other's actions, and communicate seamlessly on the court, they not only enhance their game-play but also cultivate interpersonal skills vital for life outside the sport. My experiences playing, working, and coaching in various countries have underscored the universality of teamwork as a fundamental value, transcending cultural differences.

Observing futsal's impact on family dynamics has been particularly enlightening. As student-athletes engage in collaborative play, the ethos of teamwork echoes beyond the court and into their homes. Parents become integral parts of this dynamic, supporting their children's passion for futsal and participating in the after-school experience. This collaborative effort reinforces family bonds, creating a shared sense of achievement and joy.

Culturally, the interpretation of teamwork varies, yet its essence remains universal. In Canada, I witnessed a multicultural team on the futsal court—a microcosm of a diverse society. The cultural amalgamation within the team not only enriched the game-play with varied perspectives but also fostered an environment where players learned to appreciate differences, enhancing their adaptability and social skills. The same in South Africa and the Cayman Islands, where futsal became a bridge, connecting individuals from different backgrounds in the pursuit of a shared goal.

The after-school environment, coupled with futsal training courts, plays a pivotal role in nurturing teamwork. The small, enclosed spaces create an intimate setting where communication is paramount. Students learn to rely on each other, building trust and understanding. Beyond the tangible benefits on the court, these collaborative experiences in the after-school setting become life lessons, shaping the way student-athletes navigate challenges and forge connections in their communities.

Inclusivity is a hallmark of the teamwork ethos in futsal. On the court, every player contributes, regardless of their background or skill level. This inclusivity extends into after-school programs, where diversity becomes a strength. In my coaching experiences, I have seen how students, irrespective of cultural disparities, unite through their shared love for futsal. The after-school environment becomes a melting pot where dreams are not bound by individual circumstances but are collectively pursued through collaboration and teamwork.

The collective spirit forged in after-school futsal environments extends beyond individual accomplishments, manifesting in community development. The collaborative efforts of student-athletes, families, and communities to support futsal programs create a ripple effect. In South Africa, where I coached, the after-school futsal community became a source of empowerment, bringing together diverse individuals to collectively contribute to the dreams of aspiring players.

In conclusion, this third point underscores the profound impact of teamwork in futsal, examining its role in shaping family dynamics, refining social skills, and creating collaborative communities. Drawing on experiences in culturally diverse settings, the universality of teamwork emerges as a guiding principle, not just on the court but in the broader context of life. After-school futsal environments, with their inclusive nature, serve as catalysts for teamwork, fostering an ethos where dreams are made possible through collective effort and collaboration.

5

Mastering the Clock — Time Management and Discipline:

In the intricate dance of life, futsal emerges not just as a game but as a masterclass in essential life skills. This chapter explores the profound lessons in time management and discipline that futsal imparts—skills that extend far beyond the court, influencing student-athletes, their families, and entire communities.

Futsal, with its timed constraints and swift pace, serves as a unique training ground for mastering the clock. The lessons learned on the court about urgency, precision, and the importance of each second echo in the lives of student-athletes. It's not merely about playing within the clock; it's about cultivating a mindset that values time as a precious resource. This mindset is pivotal in creating responsible individuals who understand the delicate balance between academic commitments, futsal training, and personal pursuits.

Observing the impact of futsal on time management in various countries has been enlightening. In cultures where punctuality is paramount, the timed nature of futsal aligns seamlessly with societal expectations. In contrast, cultures with a more fluid perception of time benefit from the structured nature of futsal, instilling discipline and a sense of order. This global lesson in time transcends cultural differences, emphasizing the universality of punctuality and discipline as foundational virtues.

For families and parents working the typical 9 am to 5 pm schedule, the after-school and futsal environment becomes a lifeline. The structured order of after-school nutrition, homework, and futsal training creates a framework that helps student-athletes manage their time effectively. It's not just about the skills acquired on the court but the life skills that translate into responsible time management at home. Families find a harmonious work-life balance through after-school programs, where academic priorities are met, and children engage in constructive activities that contribute to their holistic development.

The timed constraints of the futsal game translate into focus and discipline both on and off the court. Student-athletes learn to prioritize tasks, staying committed to their studies while excelling in their sporting pursuits. This dual commitment is not just a testament to their athletic abilities but also to the discipline instilled by the clock. In this process, families, communities, and nations witness the emergence of responsible individuals who understand the value of time, contributing positively to the collective fabric of society.

Cultural differences in the perception of time offer unique challenges and opportunities. Futsal, as a global sport, bridges these differences by providing a common ground where everyone respects the clock. The after-school and futsal environment becomes a microcosm of global time management, demonstrating that when everyone adheres to their designated schedule, a harmonious and productive environment ensues. It is a lesson that transcends the court, influencing how individuals interact within families, communities, and even nations.

The after-school center and futsal playing courts, thus, play a pivotal role in instilling the principles of time management and discipline. The structured routines and timed activities within these environments create a culture where punctuality, focus, and a commitment to tasks are ingrained. These habits, cultivated through the after-school and futsal experience, extend beyond the playing field, influencing how student-athletes navigate their academic pursuits, familial responsibilities, and societal engagements.

In conclusion, this fourth point highlights the invaluable lessons in time management and discipline that futsal imparts to student-athletes, families, and communities. Beyond the court, this chapter emphasizes the broader impact on work-life balance, the creation of responsible individuals, and the harmonious coexistence of diverse cultural perceptions of time. Through the after-school and futsal environments, individuals learn not just to respect the clock but to respect one another's time, contributing to a world where productivity, focus, and discipline become shared values.

6

Goal! Boosting Confidence and Self-Esteem:

In the pulsating world of futsal, the journey toward scoring goals extends beyond the mere thrill of the game. This chapter unfolds the profound transformation of young players as they not only score goals on the futsal court but also score victories boosting their confidence and self-esteem. Through the goal-oriented nature of the after-school program and futsal game and training, a shared common goal emerges—one that extends beyond the individual player to encompass their families and communities, creating a ripple effect of positive emotional development.

After-school programs and futsal training serve as goal-oriented and technical sports platforms, fostering an environment where student-athletes, families, and communities unite in a shared pursuit of success. The objectives are not only confined to winning games on the court but extend to the personal and emotional development of each participant. As a futsal character coach, I have witnessed firsthand the emotional evolution of young athletes in various countries and cultures.

Upon their first arrival at the after-school and futsal program, I often observe a mix of anticipation and trepidation in the eyes of young student-athletes. However, as they immerse themselves in the game, learn new technical skills, and achieve personal goals, a burst of smiles and confidence gradually takes hold. This positive transformation is not limited to the playing field; it radiates into their families and communities, leaving an indelible impact on the broader fabric of society.

In my coaching experiences, I have seen how the journey toward achieving personal and team goals contributes to the emotional development of young athletes. The sense of accomplishment derived from scoring goals, mastering techniques, and conquering challenges becomes a powerful catalyst for boosted confidence and self-esteem. This emotional growth is not isolated; it spills over into the individual's character, positively influencing their interactions within the after-school centers, on the futsal playing courts, and, importantly, within their families and communities.

The after-school and futsal training platform serves as a unique stage where individual accomplishments contribute to the collective success of families and communities. As young players gain confidence, their families witness a transformation in their character—becoming more resilient, positive, and well-balanced individuals. This positive energy radiates beyond the individual, creating a ripple effect that strengthens family dynamics and fosters a sense of community pride.

The impact of boosted confidence and self-esteem extends far beyond the immediate playing environment. In my early childhood playing days, futsal became a source of personal empowerment, contributing significantly to my own self-esteem and positive nature. This personal experience resonates with the observations I've made as a coach, emphasizing the enduring influence of after-school and futsal programs on emotional development.

Culturally and inclusively, the manifestation of confidence and self-esteem varies, yet the commonality lies in the positive impact on individuals, families, and communities. In South Africa, for instance, where I had the privilege of coaching, I witnessed how the collective success of student-athletes in achieving their goals elevated community spirits, and genuine love among each other. The newfound confidence in young players became a beacon of hope, inspiring others within the community to strive for their aspirations.

In conclusion, this fifth point highlights the trans-formative power of futsal in boosting confidence and self-esteem among young athletes. The goals achieved on the court transcend the game, positively influencing emotional development within the after-school centers and futsal playing courts. This emotional growth becomes a positive force that permeates families and communities, fostering a sense of pride and empowerment. After-school and futsal platforms, with their goal-oriented nature, not only shape skilled players but contribute significantly to the creation of confident, well-rounded individuals who stand as pillars in their broader societal contexts.

7

Stress-Relief Strategies — Futsal Way:

In the rhythm of daily life, futsal emerges not only as a sport but as a sanctuary—a haven of stress-relief strategies that provide a healthy outlet for the pressures of our hectic existence. This chapter uncovers the therapeutic essence of futsal, showcasing how the after-school platform becomes an expressive stage for young student-athletes, offering balance for their cognitive, physical, and emotional well-being.

For me, futsal was more than just a game; it was a lifeline that kept me grounded during my hyperactive youth. As a young student-athlete, the after-school hours were a crucial period for channeling my energy and finding focus. Playing futsal not only kept me away from potential troubles in my community but also became a means of maintaining a healthy lifestyle. I vividly remember my family doctor's advice to my parents—allowing me to engage in sports, particularly futsal after school was a prescription for managing my hyperactivity and promoting overall well-being.

As a coach in the early childhood education (ECE) field, I observed the profound impact of sports, especially futsal, on children, including those on the spectrum. Sports emerged as a passion for many of these kids, providing a therapeutic avenue for expression and stress relief. The structured nature of the futsal training platform and after-school programs became instrumental in helping children with different challenges find balance, express themselves, and receive the necessary support that they deserve.

In the context of working-class parents facing the 9 am to 5 pm grind, the after-school and futsal environment plays a pivotal role in maintaining family balance. This is not just a relief strategy for the student-athlete but for the entire family dynamic. During my coaching days in South Africa, the Cayman Islands, and Canada, I witnessed the joy and relief on the faces of parents as they picked up their children from futsal after-school programs. It was more than just a win for the student-athlete; it was a win for the working-class parents, the families, and the community as a whole.

Allowing children, whether on the spectrum or not, to engage in after-school sports like futsal is a win-win situation. It provides them with a constructive outlet to channel their energy, express stress, and find joy. The benefits extend beyond the individual, radiating positively into families, communities, and the broader societal fabric. It's a preventive strategy—let them play, help them play, and witness the transformation of pent-up energy into joy rather than letting it manifest in destructive ways within families and society.

As a nation, we collectively benefit when we prioritize the well-being of our youth through after-school and futsal programs. The stress-relief strategies embedded in these activities contribute not only to the physical health of student-athletes but also to their mental and emotional well-being. A nation that values the holistic development of its youths, invests in their after-school experiences, recognizing the enduring impact on family dynamics, community cohesion, and the overall health of society.

In conclusion, this sixth celebrates the stress-relief strategies inherent in futsal, emphasizing the positive impact on student-athletes, working-class parents, families, communities, and society at large. The after-school and futsal platform becomes a stage for expression, joy, and relief, creating a win-win situation for everyone involved. It's a call to action—let them play, help them play, for in their play lies not just individual well-being but the collective health and resilience of our families, communities, and nations.

8

Safe, Sound — Supervised Futsal Fun:

In the realm of after-school futsal, the paramount principle is safety. This chapter delves into the meticulous supervision that defines futsal sessions, ensuring a secure and enjoyable environment for young athletes. As a responsible coaching movement advocate, I staunchly advocate for the immersive benefits of safe sports within the after-school training center. Drawing on my experiences in the early childhood education (ECE) field, where safety is sacrosanct, this chapter explores how the safety net of supervised futsal programs becomes a foundation for the well-being of student-athletes, working-class parents, families, and communities.

The essence, goals, and vision of an after-school futsal center are inherently rooted in safety. Safety is not just a byproduct; it's an organic and foundational element that ensures the holistic development of every child engaged in futsal activities. As a coach, I understand the responsibility of creating an environment where parents working the 9-5 pm shift can confidently believe that their children are not only enjoying futsal but are also under the vigilant eye of responsible supervisors.

From a community perspective, the after-school futsal environment functions as a safety nest. It's a place where the rule of two in safe sports is practiced, where responsible coaching principles are embraced, and where a unique supervisory platform ensures the safety of children and student-athletes when their parents are still at work. The after-school futsal center becomes a crucial umbrella, offering shelter and structure for our youth during the vulnerable hours when they might otherwise be unsupervised at home.

Safety in the after-school futsal environment is not just about physical well-being; it extends to mental health, character development, and the overall family dynamic. The secure and sound nature of the environment provides a canvas for children to learn about safety, not just for themselves but for others as well. It becomes a platform for fostering a culture of responsibility, respect, and mutual care among the youth, contributing positively to their mental well-being.

For parents working the 9-5 pm shift, the assurance of a safe, well-supervised after-school and futsal program is invaluable. It provides them with peace of mind, knowing that their children are engaged in constructive and secure activities. The family dynamic breathes easier when safety is a core value within the after-school futsal center. It becomes a place where children can freely and organically explore, learn, and play under the watchful eye of responsible supervisors.

The after-school futsal environment is a unique platform for sustained safety initiatives. It goes beyond creating a safe space; it sustains and reinforces safety as a core value for individuals, families, communities, and society as a whole. The structured nature of after-school futsal not only builds a safety net for the individual but also contributes to the establishment of safety and structure within the family dynamic and broader community safety initiatives.

The safety-conscious nature of an after-school futsal program extends into character development. As children and student-athletes are supervised in a secure environment, their characters are unconsciously shaped by the principles of safety, responsibility, and respect. This positive influence ripples through families and communities, creating a culture where safety is not just a set of rules but a way of life.

In summary, this seventh point underscores the significance of safety in the after-school futsal environment. It serves as a beacon for responsible coaching, safe sports practices, and a unique supervisory platform for families and communities. The safety net created by after-school futsal programs goes beyond physical well-being, impacting mental health, character development, and the overall family dynamic. It becomes a sustained initiative that nurtures safety as a core value, fostering a culture of responsibility and respect within our youth, families, and communities.

9

United in Play — Futsal and Community Engagement:

In the realm of futsal and after-school programs, the influence of play extends far beyond individual enjoyment. This chapter explores how futsal becomes a catalyst for community engagement and unity, fostering connections and relationships that ripple through families, communities, and society. As student-athletes unite in play, the after-school platform becomes a hub for building friendships, trust, and a shared support network among working-class 9-5 pm parents.

Futsal and the after-school platform are not merely about individual skill development; they are powerful conduits for community engagement. The joy of play encourages student-athletes to connect, forging bonds that extend beyond the futsal playing courts. As they dribble, pass, and score goals together, a sense of unity blossoms, laying the groundwork for a vibrant community spirit.

The after-school environment becomes a melting pot where student-athletes from diverse backgrounds converge. In this space, parents working the 9-5 pm shift find common ground, connecting and building friendships with other working-class parents. The after-school center becomes more than just a pickup point for children; it transforms into a community hub where individuals unconsciously engage and build connections. The shared experience of watching their children play, fosters a sense of camaraderie among parents, breaking down barriers and nurturing a supportive community.

The unity cultivated within the futsal playing courts and after-school activities doesn't remain confined to these spaces. Student-athletes carry the lessons of teamwork, cooperation, and unity into their families and communities. The after-school platform catalyzes community-building, where the bonds forged on the futsal court extend to family dynamics and societal interactions. The platform creates a ripple effect, uniting families, friends, and neighbors in a shared sense of purpose and joy.

The close-knit nature of futsal plays a crucial role in quickly building community engagement organically. The after-school center, with its focus on skill development, teamwork, and shared experiences, becomes a microcosm of a united community. Through play, individuals discover common goals and visions, aligning themselves with the gap serviced for working-class parents. The after-school and futsal environment becomes a solution that breathes life into a united community, where everyone plays for a common goal through one platform.

Community engagement through futsal and after-school activities isn't just about joyous play; it's about building a supportive network. As families, student-athletes, and working-class parents come together in this shared space, trust is built, friendships are forged, and a network of support emerges. The after-school platform becomes a unique space where everyone, irrespective of background or role, contributes to the collective well-being of the community.

The unity fostered through futsal and after-school activities is a powerful solution for building resilient communities. In a world where individuals often lead busy lives, the after-school center serves as a meeting point where people joyfully unite, help each other, and collectively contribute to the community's success. It becomes a space where the values learned on the futsal court—teamwork, cooperation, and mutual support—translate into positive actions within families, communities, and society.

In summary, this eighth point celebrates the trans-formative power of futsal and after-school programs in fostering community engagement and unity. The joy of play serves as a bridge that connects student-athletes, parents, and the broader community. The after-school platform becomes a hub where individuals joyfully unite, build trust, and help each other, creating a strong foundation for resilient and supportive communities. Through play, the after-school and futsal environment breathe life into common goals and visions, nurturing a shared sense of purpose and joy that extends far beyond the playing field.

10

Pathway to Greatness — Talent Identification through Futsal:

Within the realm of futsal, a unique platform for talent identification unfolds, paving the way for aspiring athletes to journey towards greatness. This chapter explores how futsal not only creates pathways for athletic success but also serves as a conduit for identifying and addressing challenges within working-class 9-5 pm family dynamics. The after-school programs, in collaboration with futsal, become a trans-formative space where student-athletes are recognized, guided, and supported in their dual pursuits of education and athletics.

Futsal is more than a game; it's a pathway to greatness. Beyond being a standalone sport, futsal creates a unique trajectory for aspiring athletes. It serves as a training ground not only for futsal but also as a pathway to becoming a better soccer player. The technical skills, agility, and quick decision-making honed on the futsal court seamlessly transition into the larger soccer field, creating well-rounded athletes.

The after-school programs play a pivotal role in identifying and nurturing student-athletes. These programs become platforms for recognizing talent, not just in sports but also in academic and personal growth. As students engage in futsal and after-school activities, their unique talents and potentials are unveiled, creating pathways for them to excel not only in sports but also in their overall development.

The pathways to greatness extend beyond the individual athlete; they encompass the family dynamics of working-class parents. The after-school environment becomes a lens through which challenges faced by these families are identified. The after-school platform, with its dual emphasis on education and sports, becomes a space where the community can relate to the challenges faced by 9-5 pm working-class families.

Through intentional or unconscious efforts, the after-school futsal centers become hubs for identifying challenges and creating better pathways for student-athletes and their families. As communities engage with these families, a supportive network emerges. The after-school programs become more than a space for talent identification; they become catalysts for addressing the needs of families and fostering their journey to greatness and success.

The after-school futsal centers serve as sustainable pipelines for identifying athletic talents. Like a garden where seeds are discovered, nurtured, and cultivated, these centers become the breeding ground for budding athletes. Through systematic training, guidance, and support, the talents discovered in these programs have the potential to blossom into impactful contributors to their communities, cities, and nations.

As the after-school futsal platform monitors and guides talented student-athletes, it becomes a trans-formative space where individuals discover their truest selves. The journey to greatness isn't just about excelling in sports; it's about becoming individuals who positively influence their communities and society as a whole. The after-school and futsal environment becomes a dynamic force that diffuses greatness beyond the playing field.

In a nutshell, this ninth point celebrates the multifaceted role of futsal and after-school programs as pathways to greatness. It explores how futsal serves as a unique platform for talent identification, creating trajectories for aspiring athletes to excel not only in sports but also in education and personal growth. The after-school centers become trans-formative spaces that identify challenges within working-class family dynamics, offering support and fostering the journey to greatness for both student-athletes and their families. It's a celebration of the potential that lies within these programs to shape individuals, families, communities, and society at large.

11

Affordable Adventures — Futsal for Every Budget:

In the landscape of organized sports, futsal emerges as an accessible adventure for every budget, contrary to prevailing misconceptions. This chapter uncovers how futsal provides an affordable avenue for children to engage in organized sports, particularly within the inclusive framework of after-school programs. It sheds light on the gap that working-class parents face and emphasizes why investments from communities, cities, nations, corporations, employers, and governments are crucial to making after-school futsal services affordable for all.

Futsal's affordability is a key aspect that often goes unnoticed. Within the after-school program platform, it becomes an inclusive hub where every child, regardless of their socioeconomic background, can participate in the joy of playing sports. The misconception that organized sports are financially burdensome is dispelled, as futsal becomes a sport that bridges economic gaps and welcomes children from every walk of life.

Investing in after-school futsal programs is not just about making sports accessible; it's a strategic move that can save communities, governments, employers, and nations economically. By investing in prevention through affordable after-school futsal services, communities can potentially reduce the strain on healthcare, social services, and rehabilitation programs that may be required if preventative measures are ignored. It's a shift from investing in a cure to investing in the health and well-being of the future generation.

Affordability in after-school futsal is paramount, not just for the children and student-athletes but also for their working-class parents. The after-school environment becomes a haven for the parents, assuring them that their children are not only safe and healthy but are also engaged in constructive and affordable activities. After-school futsal centers contribute to the overall happiness of working parents, fostering a positive work environment and a thriving economy.

Investing in affordable after-school futsal programs is an investment in the human potential and resources of the future. By making these programs accessible to all families, communities are nurturing the foundation of their nations. After-school and futsal programs become more than just sports activities; they are investments into the health and wellness of families, which collectively shape the fabric and core of a nation.

For a working-class parent, knowing that their children are safe, healthy, and engaged in after-school futsal activities is more than a relief—it's an investment in sustaining a quality workforce and a robust economy. The positive impact of affordable after-school futsal extends beyond the immediate benefits for families; it influences the broader community and contributes to a harmonious society.

Affordability is not just about reducing the cost of participation; it's about breaking down barriers. When after-school futsal programs are accessible to every child and family, it creates a ripple effect that transcends economic considerations. As children from diverse backgrounds come together to play, learn, and grow, societal barriers are dismantled, fostering unity, understanding, and a shared sense of community.

And finally, this tenth point advocates for the affordability of after-school futsal adventures for every budget. It highlights the misconceptions surrounding the cost of organized sports and emphasizes the inclusive nature of futsal within after-school programs. The chapter underscores the economic benefits of investing in prevention through affordable after-school futsal services and the positive impact it has on families, communities, and nations. Ultimately, making after-school futsal accessible to all is an investment in a strong, joyful, and united community where barriers vanish, and everyone can play and experience the fun of futsal.

12

Conclusion:

As we bring this enlightening journey to a close, this guide transcends the realm of mere love for futsal, offering a comprehensive approach to after-school sports. It serves as a blueprint for parents, coaches, and communities, illustrating how futsal can be the transformative force that empowers and brings joy. Welcome to a world where futsal serves as the bridge, nurturing talents, and sparking a passion that extends far beyond the boundaries of the court.

In these pages, we've explored not just the game itself, but the 10 ways in which futsal empowers working-class parents and student-athletes alike. It stands as a revolution in after-school routines, addressing the challenges faced by families and communities. Futsal becomes the solution and answers to the unsupervised gap in the family dynamic structure, offering a remedy through carefully crafted after-school futsal services and programs.

Drawing on childhood experiences and humble observations, we've embarked on a journey toward building stronger families, communities, and societies. Futsal, in its essence, is more than just fun—it's a powerful tool for shaping the future of our student-athletes. It goes beyond the joy of playing a game; it encapsulates the joy of learning, growing, and succeeding within a supportive and empowering environment.

As we reflect on the transformative power of futsal, let us recognize the profound impact it has on the lives of working-class parents and their children. It's not just a sport; it's a remedy for the challenges faced by families working the 9-5 pm shift. Through after-school futsal programs, parents can rest assured that their children are not only engaged but are also thriving in a safe, supervised, and enjoyable environment.

Futsal, as presented in this guide, is a unifying force that transcends individual achievements. It brings communities together, creating a shared vision and purpose. It builds trust, fosters friendships, and forms a strong support network. In the heart of the futsal court and the after-school environment, the seeds of unity are sown, flourishing into a robust sense of community that extends far beyond the playing field.

As we bid farewell to this guide, let us carry forward the lessons learned, and the inspiration gained. Let us champion the cause of after-school futsal programs, recognizing them as invaluable investments in the well-being and future of our youth. In the joy of futsal, we find not only a game but a pathway to empowerment, enjoyment, and a brighter future for working-class parents, student-athletes, families, and communities.

Futsal is fun for us all, and in its fun, we discover a force that can reshape, rejuvenate, and unify. Welcome to a world where futsal becomes a beacon of joy, empowerment, and transformation—a world

CONCLUSION:

where families, communities, and societies flourish through the shared passion for the beautiful game.

Your feedback is invaluable – share your thoughts and reviews to inspire continued growth and excellence in the realm of after-school futsal sports.

Thank you for being part of this journey.

13

Resources + Acknowledgment:

- NearChukwu. (1 C.E., June 19). *NearChukwu*. NearChukwu. Retrieved January 27, 2024, from https://www.nearchukwu.com/
- Innocenti, U. O. O. R.-. (n.d.). *Playing the Game: A framework for successful child-focused sport for development programs*. (C)2024 www.unicef-irc.org - UNICEF Office of Research - Innocenti. Retrieved January 27, 2024, from https://www.unicef-irc.org/playing-the-game
- Coatsworth, J. D., & Conroy, D. E. (2007). Youth sports as a component of organized after-school programs. *New Directions for Youth Development, 2007*(115), 57–74. https://doi.org/10.1002/yd.223
- Halpern, R. (1999). After-School Programs for Low-Income Children: Promise and challenges. *The Future of Children, 9*(2), 81. https://doi.org/10.2307/1602708
- Bradshaw, J. (2015). Child Poverty and Child Well-Being in International Perspective. In *Children's well-being* (pp. 59–70). https://doi.org/10.1007/978-3-319-17506-5_4
- Burchinal, M. (2017). Measuring early care and education quality.

Child Development Perspectives, 12(1), 3–9. https://doi.org/10.1111/cdep.12260

- *Sport Safety | Coach.* (n.d.-b). Retrieved January 27, 2024, from https://coach.ca/sport-safety
- Contributeurs aux projets Wikimedia. (2023, November 13). *Juan Carlos Ceriani Gravier.* Retrieved January 27, 2024, from https://fr.wikipedia.org/wiki/Juan_Carlos_Ceriani_Gravier
- Chartrand, J. M., & Lent, R. W. (1987). Sports Counseling: Enhancing the development of the Student-Athlete. *Journal of Counseling & Development, 66*(4), 164–167. https://doi.org/10.1002/j.1556-6676.1987.tb00837.x

About the Author

Anistetus Nonso Dike, also known as NearChukwu, resides in Canada with his family and is a visionary Futsal Character Coach and creative designer with 15+ years of experience in the arts, sports, and Early Childhood Education fields. Having worked globally and predominantly in school-age after-school art and sports programs across diverse communities, he has garnered humbling experiences and absorbed unique cultures along the way. Passionate about the game of futsal, a lifelong learner, and grateful for his parents, teachers, and mentors. NearChukwu dedicates himself to fostering resilience and unity in families, student-athletes, and communities through the transformative influence of futsal and purpose-driven design.

You can connect with me on:

🌐 https://www.linkedin.com/in/nondyk

🖇 https://www.instagram.com/nearchukwu

Subscribe to my newsletter:

✉ https://nearchukwu.com/contact-us